How To
Oust A King

An Enlightening Tale of Defeating Corrupt Leadership
& Final Wake-Up Call for America

By

Scott Killian

Written, illustrated and published by Scott Killian
ISBN# 978-0-692-50012-5

Bible scriptures from World English Bible (public domain).

For further information, go to **OustAKing.com**.
Also see Facebook, Twitter, Instagram, YouTube and more.

E-mail inquiries to **Info@OustAKing.com** or through website above (Contact).

To receive e-mail updates or related information, send your e-mail address to **Subscribe@OustAKing.com** or through website above (Contact).

For speaking engagements, radio/TV discussions or other public events, please e-mail requests to **Events@OustAKing.com** or through website above (Contact).

Truth

vs.

Deception

O nce upon a time in a land of milk and honey,
were a proud people who wanted a new king
to help with their needs, desires and burden of money.

The system of vote carried forward from the past, revealed confusion, misrepresentation and division great and vast.

Expensive campaigns were thrown to and fro,
hype and no selection were predominant,
leading to public woe.

Amid the confusion a king was finally elected,
dreams of hope and change finally resurrected.

"HIP HIP HOORAY! PROSPERITY IS ON THE WAY!"

The King and his courts began to reign
with uplifting promises and word,
but it wasn't long before a lack of results
became tragic, even absurd.

Promises of jobs, healthcare and perks
without limit, only smoke screens of politics,
socialism and other self-serving gimmicks.

What the King and the courts said in words
they did not do,
lies of destruction were rampant
through and through....

Taxes, inflation and oppressive control
became so heavy a load,
freedom and everyday living were about to implode.

"What should we do?" the people cried,
tired of bondage and the curse of being pushed aside.

The majority in fear said nothing at all,
only silently thinking,
"I'm looking out for myself so I don't fall."

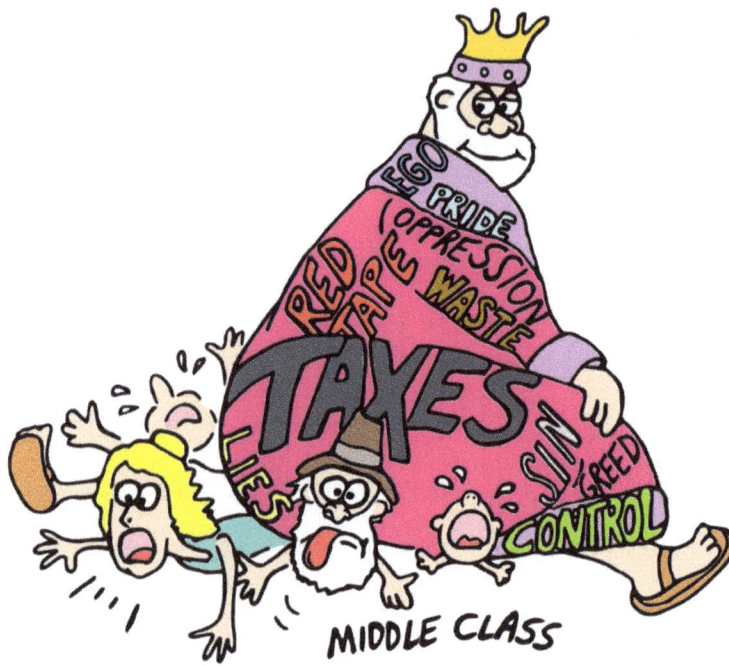

MIDDLE CLASS

NOT MY PROBLEM!

GUESS I'LL HAVE TO EXTORT, I MEAN "MAKE" MORE MONEY

ONLY THE STRONG SURVIVE

BETTER NOT MAKE ANY WAVES, I COULD LOSE MY JOB!

AS LONG AS I GET MY PAYCHECK, EVERYTHING IS FINE!

"SOUNDS LIKE AN "I" PROBLEM"

So many had gifts that could have formed solutions,
but selfishly never bothered because deep down
they knew the cost of revolution.

Round and round the people bickered and
complained,
going nowhere with words,
enough to make a wise man insane.

They were about to lose everything they've ever
worked for by not taking a stand,
ousting the King and his courts was the
only true option,
most positions better off left unmanned.

Evil prospered through the King and his courts
because of one simple reason,
good people did nothing about it, which is
essentially **treason**.

After years of oppression, silence and
underlying debate,
a youth of small stature finally spoke out in public
and did not hesitate.

"Why not do the obvious, resist and start to **unite**?"
but most kept quiet for fear of confrontation
and the simple feeling of fright.

Several offended shouted,
"What's the point when so many do not care?
I'll do my part but nobody will do theirs!"

13

The youth spoke boldly once again.
"Do you care enough to truly unite yourself
or will you continue to pull another selfish excuse
off the endless shelf?"

The naysayers scorned,
"It'll never work, nobody will ever agree.
It's too big, too late, we have no leader,
not enough money, impossible....don't you see?!"

The older crowd rebuked the youth
with resistance to no avail,
stubborn to the fact that their prideful denial,
unwillingness to change and foolish choices
were why they would continue to fail.

Deep down they all knew they could arrive
at a number of solutions,
but they were unwilling to hear and search for **truth**,
blinded by their selfish delusions.

Some acknowledged the responsibility of
having to act and prove,
but most chose to remain weak "followers,"
only considering action if others made the first move.

The truth was, most did not want to
sacrifice or pay any kind of price,
to do so would admit they must repent
and change their own selfish ways,
far more than just once or twice.

Fear of losing their job, confrontation
and the pain of doing what's right,
was their choice of denying truth instead of
trusting God, stepping out in faith
and taking action to fight.

However, an unknown number in the community
were not willing to accept the slavery
of corruption and sin,
for God put it their heart to be free, victorious
and ultimately glorify Him.

Some began to unite together, pray, strategize
and seek all kinds of answers,
no longer tolerating selfishness, political correctness
or truth-avoiding dancers.

There were also some who appeared noble
to do the same in general talk,
but with selfish motives and methods,
an ill-begotten, counterfeit walk.

Both began their journey based on
what they ultimately chose to believe,
one heading toward truth,
the other ill reprieve.

It wasn't long before the King found out that many
were collaborating against him,
so he hired sellout cronies to spread false rumors
that resistance was futile and grim.

Those who wanted truth could see right through
the hype and foolish lies,
those who didn't took them hook, line and sinker,
justifying themselves at their own and everyone else's
demise.

21

Solutions to ousting the King and his courts
were not easy but quite obvious and plain,
the only thing stopping anyone was their
stubborn unwillingness, false reasoning
and denial of being vain.

The King continued to abuse his power once again
by extorting taxes, oppression, inflation, fees and fines,
but for the first time businesses and the people
refused to pay and obey
for crossing too many lines.

25

The King tried to gather police and troops
to arrest those who refused to pay,
but most police, troops and workers refused to do so,
their own people they would not betray.

For you see a king only has power over people when
people like you choose to obey, support or follow,
sell your soul for a paycheck, fear or comfort,
a bitter pill of permanent destruction
you and everyone will swallow.

Evil will only prevail
when good people choose to bail.

Unfortunately some troops sold out
and proceeded with the civil arrests,
but those contained were quickly released due to
united pressure, boycotts and persistent protests.

Boycotts, picketing, prayer, petitions and letter,
there's all kinds of creative ideas people will come up
with when they finally choose to act,
do what's required and come together.

"Leaderless" movements independent of any man,
group, leader, process or host,
uniting will coordinate automatically when enough
begin to finally do the obvious of what's needed most.

The key is to cut off the cash flow and help
of anyone corrupt,
the lifeline of their power and control
you will quickly disrupt.

Aggressively demand that they immediately
quit or resign,
otherwise quickly impeach, recall, or terminate,
do not compromise no matter the cost or time.

Shun, impede and make their lives miserable
through all kinds of public pressure and resistance,
they'll eventually leave or be kicked out
due to power in numbers and never-ending
persistence.

This includes those who support, finance or are
connected to the corrupt in any significant way,
cut off every lifeline you can
and victory will soon replace dismay.

KING'S
ATTORNEY

31

KING'S
ADMINISTRATION

You already know that with resistance
there is risk and a possible high price to pay,
but with literally everything in jeopardy already,
do not be deceived,
there simply is no other option or way.

YEAH BUT I COULD LOSE MY JOB!

OR MORE!

"WAKE UP PEOPLE!! YOU'RE ON THE VERGE OF LOSING IT ALL ANYWAY IF YOU DON'T ACT NOW!"

Success will depend on how willing you truly are
to unite, act and commit,
will you defend "all for one, one for all,"
or selfishly choose to split?

Prayer and relying on God
are foremost in being essential,
but prayer alone without repentance and
responsible action will once again miserably fail,
lacking favor providential.

"Love God and Others" (Matt 22:37-40)
are the foremost commandments we've disobeyed
by not taking this obvious action,
excuses and false justification will only lead to further
blindness, destruction and divine dissatisfaction.

Still think uniting or taking action is futile,
too risky for your job or you don't have time?
You and everyone are literally on the verge of
losing everything anyway,
selfishly denying this with inaction is equally a crime.

After all, *anyone* can talk to
and encourage someone else to unite,
demonstrating by example
true commitment, interest and readiness to act,
not giving in to selfish excuses, doubt or fright.

The movement of people against the King and the
corrupt finally freed them from extortion and slavery,
all because good people took a stand against
their own fear and selfishness,
replacing with God, love and bravery!

The people lived happily ever after, right?
Not quite.

The moral of this story goes far beyond uniting,
needs or fighting to oust a king,
it's an issue of *God*, your *heart* and *eternity*,
not a selfish or physical thing.

The people thought money, things and a king
would ultimately bring them satisfaction,
fulfilling the desires of their heart once again
produced suffering and destruction,
a completely opposite reaction.

The freedoms and true needs of life
are not found by doing what you want or
what others think at all,
God clearly warns that when we follow
our own ways or the world's,
"Pride comes before a fall" (Proverbs 16:18.)

The answer to freedom and fulfillment is not in
ourselves, money or a worldly king so many are
looking to serve,
but only through **Jesus Christ**,
the "King of All Kings" of whom none of us deserve.

This life is not about you, money, survival or pursuing
self-gratifying pleasure,
but receiving Jesus as your savior for eternity
and serving Him with your life,
of which there is no greater treasure.

Only God can intervene, empower and
change our hearts to do what's truly right,
doing it our own way, without God or with
compromise will only produce further suffering,
selfishness and plight.

Understand that everything you've ever strived
for and value in life will literally *all*
be a complete waste,
if not directed by, for and through Jesus,
Heaven and true peace you will never taste.

Do not deceive yourself. Doing good works or being a
good person will never earn you God's favor or get you
into Heaven,
it's only by receiving Jesus' free gift and turning your
life over to Him
will you ever truly be free and forgiven.

If you think this kind of thing could
never work for you,
understand it's literally the *only* answer for everyone,
what's been told for centuries has always been true.

The longer you wait to become saved by Jesus the
more deceived you will be,
to a point of "no return,"
such opportunity and truth you will no longer see.

The everyday choices you make from here on out will
determine your and many other's eternal fate,
give your life to Jesus now to find your true purpose,
before it's too late.

After all...

"One nation <u>under God</u>" is what made
this nation great!

The END
(of corruption, a new beginning in Christ!)

Salvation Prayer

Verbally confess and believe with all your heart the following:

Jesus,

I come to you today as a sinner who needs you.
I believe by faith that the Bible is true and you are
the Son of God who died and rose again for my sins.

I sincerely repent (turn away) from my life of sin and
commit to living for you instead.

I ask you to please enter my heart and become
Lord of my life in everything I do.

I thank you for your sacrifice on the cross and
allowing me to spend eternity in Heaven with You
forever!

Amen!

Congratulations! If you truly meant it,
you are saved for eternity!!

Scriptures

Love God & Others Above Yourself

• **Matthew 22:37-40** (World English Bible)

[37] Jesus said to him, 'You shall **love the Lord your God** with all your heart, with all your soul, and with all your mind.' [38] This is the first and great commandment. [39] A second likewise is this, 'You shall **love your neighbor as yourself**.' [40] The whole law and the prophets depend on these two commandments."

{This says it all. These literally are the top two commandments and priorities above everything else in life. We are not loving God or others when we allow corruption to continue to hurt others as we have done. No amount of excuses or reasoning will ever change this, only a humble and repentant heart.}

• **John 14:23-24**

[23] Jesus answered him, "**If a man loves me, he will keep my word** *{obey}*. My Father will love him, and we will come to him, and make our home with him. [24] He who doesn't love me doesn't keep my words. The word which you hear isn't mine, but the Father's who sent me.

- **Matthew 7:21**

Not everyone who says to me, 'Lord, Lord,' will enter into the Kingdom of Heaven; but he who **does** the will of my Father who is in heaven.

{Though it's not about performance in doing good works or being perfect, only those who genuinely commit to intimately know and consistently obey Jesus with a right heart are saved. Salvation is more than just saying a prayer to avoid hell or trying to be a good person. The state of this nation today demonstrates just how many people have disobeyed God and failed to know Him personally. Many who say and think they are saved likely are not.}

- **James 1:22**

But be **doers** of the word, and not only hearers, **deluding** *{deceiving}* **your own selves**.

- **James 4:17**

To him therefore who knows to do good, and doesn't do it, to him it is **sin**. *{We sin against God, others and ourselves.}*

- **Galatians 6:2**

Bear one another's burdens, and so fulfill the law of Christ.

Do Not Follow Your Own Reasoning, Feelings or Desires

- **Mark 7:21-22**

[21] For from within, out of the **hearts** of men, proceed evil thoughts, adulteries, sexual sins, murders, thefts,

[22] coveting, wickedness, **deceit**, lustful desires, an evil eye, blasphemy, **pride**, and foolishness.

{Though we all have good traits, we are still born sinners with corrupt hearts that only Jesus can change and save us from if we allow Him to.}

- **Jeremiah 17:9**

The heart is **deceitful** above all things, and it is exceedingly corrupt: who can know *{understand}* it?

{We're not nearly as "good" and truthful as we want to believe. So much so, we deceive even ourselves. Don't feel condemned about this but simply acknowledge this truth with humility, submit your whole heart to Jesus and obey Him so He can change your heart and life one day at a time.}

Do Not Follow Your Own Reasoning, Feelings or Desires

- **Proverbs 3:5-7**

[5] Trust *{faith}* in Jesus with all your heart, and **don't lean on your own understanding**. [6] In all your ways acknowledge *{submit to}* him, and he will make your paths straight. [7] Don't be wise in your own eyes. Fear *{revere, respect}* Jesus, and **depart from evil.**

- **Isaiah 55:8-9**

[8] "For my thoughts are not your thoughts, and your ways are not my ways," says the Lord. [9] "For as the heavens are higher than the earth, so are my ways higher than your ways, and my thoughts than your thoughts.

{His ways and understanding are far above ours. Accept them in faith.}

- **Proverbs 16:25**

[25] There is a way which seems right to a man, but in the end it leads to **death.**

{This says it all. God's ways work and ours don't as history proves time and time again. No matter how confident we think we are about knowing something, only God is perfect to know all truth. That is why we are commanded to full trust, rely on and obey in <u>faith</u> according to what God says instead of what we understand or want to believe.}

60

- **Hebrews 11:6**

Without **faith** *{fully trusting in God}* it is impossible to be well pleasing to him, for he who comes to God must believe that he exists, and that he is a rewarder of those who seek him.

{You will only find Jesus and the truth by trusting and pursuing Him with your whole heart, not through understanding or reasoning.}

Do Not Follow Other People, Leaders or the Ways of the World

- **1 John 2:15-17**

[15] Do not love the world or the things that are in the world. If anyone loves the world, the Father's love isn't in him. [16] For all that is in the world, the **lust of the flesh,** the **lust of the eyes,** and the **pride of life,** isn't the Father's, but is the world's. [17] The world is **passing away** with its lusts, but he who does God's will remains **forever.** *{You can't follow God and the world both. You must choose one or the other.}*

- **Romans 12:2**

Do not be conformed to this world, but be transformed by the **renewing of your mind** {*we must change our thinking to God's ways*}, so that you may prove what is the good, well-pleasing, and perfect will of God.

{*History has proven time and time again that man does not have the answers to life or the solutions to this nation's problems. Truth, discernment and wisdom only come from the Lord when we truly humble ourselves and submit to Him.*}

- **John 4:24**

God is spirit, and those who worship him must worship in **spirit** and **truth**."

{*You cannot receive truth and wisdom from the Holy Spirit until you are saved by Jesus. If you're not obeying with a right heart, you're not truly following Jesus in spirit and in truth.*}

Do Not Follow After Money, Man's Approval or Compromise for a Paycheck

• **1 Timothy 6:9-12**

[9] But those who are determined to be rich fall into a temptation and a snare and many foolish and harmful lusts, such as drown men in ruin and destruction. [10] For the **love of money** is a root of all kinds of evil. Some have been led astray from the faith in their greed, and have pierced themselves through with many sorrows. [11] But you, man of God, **flee these things, and follow after righteousness, godliness, faith, love, patience, and gentleness**. [12] Fight the good fight of faith. Take hold of the **eternal life** to which you were called, and you confessed the good confession in the sight of many witnesses.

• **Hebrews 13:5**

Be free from the **love of money**, content with such things as you have, for he has said, "I will in no way leave you, neither will I in any way forsake you."

{God will take care of our needs when we truly put Him first. We are loving money and ourselves when we put making a living <u>ahead</u> of God or the needs of others.}

Do Not Follow After Money, Man's Approval
or Compromise for a Paycheck

- **Matthew 6:24**

"No one can serve two masters, for either he will hate the one and love the other; or else he will be devoted to one and despise the other. **You cannot serve both God and Mammon** {*money*}.

{*Money itself is not bad but the love, greed and compromises made for money (including material possessions, success, acceptance, security, control, etc.) are why this nation is falling to permanent destruction. Again, you can't have it both ways. You must choose one or the other. God has a far better plan than you surviving by your own efforts or achieving your own desires through money.*}

- **Proverbs 11:18**

Wicked people earn **deceitful wages,** but one who sows righteousness reaps a sure reward {*especially for eternity*}.

- **Galatians 1:10**

For am I now seeking the **favor of men** {*for money, recognition, etc.*}, or of God? Or am I striving to **please men**? For if I were still pleasing men, I would <u>not</u> be a servant of Christ.

*Do Not Follow After Money, Man's Approval
or Compromise for a Paycheck*

- **John 12:43**

for they loved men's praise more than God's praise.

- **Jeremiah 17:5**

Jesus says: Cursed is the man who **trusts in man**, and makes flesh his arm *{relies on his own strength}*, and whose heart departs from the Lord.

- **Ephesians 4:28**

Let him who stole **steal no more**; but rather let him labor, producing with his hands **something that is good**, that he may have something to **give to him who has need**. *{God wants us to conduct work or employment that truly helps others and glorifies Him rather than steal, compromise or settle for a paycheck. Mostly looking out for yourself instead of others, using others to get what you want, playing political games to keep your job, being dishonest, manipulative, wasteful, accepting corruption, not speaking up or confronting management, giving in to unjustified fear for your job, taking or remaining in a job because of money without trying to find something better, not waiting on God and countless other forms of selfish agendas and compromise directly violate God's foremost commands to love Him (by obeying) and others.}*

*Do Not Follow After Money, Man's Approval
or Compromise for a Paycheck*

- **Proverbs 29:26**

Many seek the ruler's *{king, leader, boss, etc.}* favor, but a man's justice comes from the Lord.

- **Colossians 3:23-24**

[23] And whatever you do, work heartily, as **for the Lord**, and **not for men**, [24] knowing that from the Lord you will receive the reward of the inheritance; for you serve the Lord Christ. *{The vicious, destructive cycle of sin that makes employment such a burden will only diminish when we truly decide to work for the Lord instead of ourselves and other people.}*

Repent (Turn to God & Away from Sin)

- **2 Chronicles 7:14**

[14] if my people *{Christians}*, who are called by my name, shall humble themselves, and pray, and seek my face, and **turn from their wicked ways;** *then* I will hear from heaven, and will forgive their sin, and will heal their land. *{This nation is not recovering because we are not repenting.}*

Why Aren't We Repenting?

- **Proverbs 16:18**

Pride goes before destruction, and a haughty spirit before a fall.

{This is the root of our problems....foolish pride! True humility and submission to God are essential. If you stubbornly choose to follow what you want or think is right instead of the truth (Jesus and His ways), you will inevitably fall to destruction in this life and especially the eternal one to come. The consequences are eternal.}

- **Psalm 53:1**

The **fool** has said in his heart, "There is no God." They are **corrupt**, and have done abominable iniquity.

- **Proverbs 28:26**

One who **trusts in himself** is a **fool**; but one who walks in wisdom *{God's wisdom, not man's or our own}* is kept safe.

- **Psalm 10:4**

The wicked, in the **pride** of his face, has **no room in his thoughts for God.**

Why Aren't We Repenting?

- **James 4:6**

But he gives more grace. Therefore it says, **"God resists the proud**, but gives grace to the humble."

{Precisely why things are not improving in this country. God will only help the humble, not the proud.}

- **Galatians 6:3**

For if a man thinks himself to be something when he is nothing *{right in his or her own eyes, in control, smart enough to manage things on their own, etc.}*, he **deceives himself.**

{The tremendous danger of pride is that you don't even know you are deceived!}

- **Galatians 5:17**

For the flesh *{mind, feelings, physical senses}* lusts against the Spirit *{God's inner presence, strength, guidance}*, and the Spirit against the flesh; and these are **contrary to one another,** that you may <u>**not**</u> **do the things that you desire.**

{Life is about choosing Jesus and His ways instead of pleasing the fleshly desires of our sin nature. We are all fighting a spiritual battle, a marathon war for your and everyone's eternal soul that can only be won through Jesus.}

Why Aren't We Repenting?

- **Jeremiah 17:23**

But they **did not listen**, neither turn their ear, but made their **neck stiff**, that they might **not hear** *{refused to listen to the truth}*, and might **not receive instruction** *{refused to be corrected}*.

{Again, the root reason why this nation is falling to permanent destruction....stubborn pride!}

- **Acts 7:51**

"You **stiff-necked** and uncircumcised in heart and ears, you always resist the Holy Spirit! As your fathers did, so you do. *{History repeats itself only if we allow it to.}*

- **Deuteronomy 9:6**

Know therefore, that the Lord your God does not give you this good land to possess for your righteousness; for you are a **stiff-necked people**.

{The good in this nation continues because of God's grace, mercy and will, not our acts of righteousness as if we own, earned, deserve or are entitled to it. That's nothing but foolish pride.}

• **2 Chronicles 36:13**

He *{King Zedekiah of Judah}* also rebelled against king Nebuchadnezzar, who had made him swear by God: but he **stiffened his neck**, and **hardened his heart against turning to Jesus**, the God of Israel.

{Just like this nation today.}

• **Deuteronomy 8:20**

As the nations that the Lord makes to perish before you, so you shall perish; because **you would not listen to the Lord your God's voice.** *{The choice is entirely up to us.}*

Unite

• **Ephesians 4:25**

Therefore putting away falsehood, **speak truth** each one with his neighbor. For **we are members of one another.** *{God designed us to be an essential part of one body in Christ where we all highly affect and depend on one another. When we go against this, there are severe and eternal consequences. We are not "independent" as we would like to believe.}*

Unite

- **Romans 12:5**

so we, who are many, are **one body** in Christ, and individually members one of another. *{The choice to honor God and others as one body or be selfish is entirely up to us.}*

- **Philippians 2:1-4**

[1] If there is therefore any exhortation in Christ, if any consolation of love, if any fellowship of the Spirit, if any tender mercies and compassion, [2] make my joy full, by being **like-minded**, having the **same love**, being of **one accord, of one mind;** [3] doing nothing through rivalry or through conceit, but in **humility, each counting others better than himself;** [4] each of you not just looking to his own things, but each of you also **to the things of others**.
{Today's "every man for himself" mentality goes against God's design and is a selfish, losing game for everybody as we are seeing today. We should be loving, helping and looking out for one another instead. Uniting is necessary to conquer evil.}

- **Ecclesiastes 4:12**

If a man prevails against one who is alone, two shall withstand him; and a threefold cord is not quickly broken.
{Power in numbers. God offers an anointing of power when two or more gather in His name as well.}

Unite

- **1 Corinthians 12:26**

When **one member suffers, all the members suffer with it.** Or when one member is honored, all the members rejoice with it. *{When you or others choose to sin, it directly and indirectly causes suffering and spiritual destruction upon yourself and literally <u>everyone else</u> whether you see the connection or not. We are sinning against Jesus himself, others and ourselves.}*

Stand Firm Against Corruption, Evil, Satan

- **James 4:7**

Be subject therefore *{submit}* to God. But **resist** the devil, and he will flee from you. *{Submit to God first, then resist.}*

- **Ephesians 5:11**

Have no fellowship with the unfruitful deeds of darkness, but rather **reprove** *{disapprove, censure, expose}* **them.**

- **Psalm 94:16**

Who will rise up for me against the wicked? Who will stand up for me against the evildoers?

- ## Ephesians 6:13

Therefore put on the whole armor of God, that you may be able to **withstand** in the evil day, and, having done all, to **stand**. *{We are fighting a spiritual, marathon war.}*

- ## Acts 5:29

But Peter and the apostles answered, "We must **obey God rather than men**."

It's Not About You or This Life

- ## Matthew 16:26-27

[26] For **what will it profit a man, if he gains the whole world, and forfeits his life** *{eternal future}*? Or what will a man give in exchange for his life *{eternal future}*? [27] For the Son of Man will come in the glory of his Father with his angels, and then he will render to everyone according to his deeds.

{This clearly says it all. You gain absolutely nothing if you sacrifice your eternal future for the fleeting pleasures of this temporary life.}

It's Not About You or This Life

- **Galatians 6:7-9**

[7] **Do not be deceived.** God is not mocked, for **whatever a man sows, that he will also reap**. [8] For he who sows to his own **flesh** will from the flesh reap **corruption**. But he who sows to the **Spirit** will from the Spirit reap **eternal life**. [9] Let us not be weary in doing good, for we will reap in due season, if we **do not give up**. *{This country is reaping destruction because of what so many have sown over the years. The consequences will be eternal for those who do not truly repent and turn their life over to Jesus.}*

- **James 4:14**

Whereas you don't know what your life will be like tomorrow. For what is your life? For you are a **vapor**, that appears for a little time, and then vanishes away.

{People become overly focused on happiness and this fleeting life rather than preparing for the far more important eternal one to come.}

- **Hebrews 9:27**

Inasmuch as it is appointed for men to **die once**, and after this, **judgment**, *{You only get one shot throughout this life to get saved and fulfill God's will and purpose. After that, there are no second chances. Your choices will affect eternity forever.}*

74

It's Not About You or This Life

- **Revelation 20:15**

If anyone was not found written in the book of life *{saved by Jesus}*, he was cast into the **lake of fire.**

- **Colossians 3:2**

Set your mind *{what you think about and pursue}* on the things that are **above** *{eternal}*, not on the things that are on the earth.

- **Matthew 6:19-21**

[19] "Do not lay up treasures for yourselves on the earth, where moth and rust consume, and where thieves break through and steal; [20] but lay up for yourselves treasures in **heaven** *{eternity}*, where neither moth nor rust consume, and where thieves don't break through and steal; [21] for where your treasure is, there your heart will be also.

{Our heart's treasures (priorities) and focus should be in Jesus himself who is the truth and only way to eternal life. Choose Him, choose life and reap eternal treasures in Heaven forever.}

God Has a Specific Plan for Your Life. Follow Him, Not Your Own Desires or the World

- **Jeremiah 29:11-13**

[11] For I know the thoughts that I think toward you, says the Lord, thoughts of **peace**, and not of evil, to give you **hope and a future**. [12] You shall call on me, and you shall go and pray to me, and I will listen to you. [13] You shall seek me, **and find me, when you search for me with <u>all</u> your heart**.

- **Galatians 2:20**

I have been crucified with Christ, and it is no longer I that live, but Christ living in me. That life which I now live in the flesh, I live by **faith** {trust} in the Son of God, who loved me, and gave himself up for me.

{God has a wonderful plan for you but only if you surrender your will and desires to Him. You live life on His terms and direction, not yours.}

Jesus Is the Only Way to Heaven, the Only True Solution to Our Problems

- John 3:16

For God so loved the world, that he gave his one and only Son, that whoever **believes in him should not perish, but have eternal life**.

- Acts 4:12

There is salvation in **no other**, for neither is there any other name under heaven, that is given among men, by which we must be **saved**!"

Jesus Is the Only Way to Heaven,
the Only True Solution to Our Problems

- ### John 14:6

Jesus said to him, **"I am the way, the truth, and the life. No one comes to the Father, except through me.**

*{There is literally only one way to ever recognize and arrive at the truth concerning your eternal future and overcoming problems in this life......Jesus. We can never be saved or gain God's favor by doing good works or being a good person. Only the blood of Jesus can cleanse our sins to be in the presence of a pure and holy God for eternity. Only the blood of Jesus can pay the price for you and others to receive the grace, mercy and favor of God in this life and the far more important eternal one to come. Jesus loves us so much that He died a horrible death on the cross for **You** and everyone so we could spend eternity with Him and God forever. Though we deserve nothing, He gave everything out of pure, unconditional love. Will you receive the free gift He suffered for before it's too late?}*

One day soon
every knee will bow and
every tongue will confess that
Jesus Christ is Lord!

Philippians 2:9-11

This book will only be as effective as the number of people you share and encourage it with along with your own personal, everyday choices. The future of this country and true change through a united movement in Christ are dependent upon *You.* Thank you for your love, support, involvement and courage! May Jesus be glorified according to His specific will and purpose for your life!

Index

For further information, go to **OustAKing.com**.
Also see Facebook, Twitter, Instagram, YouTube and more.

E-mail inquiries to **Info@OustAKing.com** or through website above (Contact).

To receive e-mail updates or related information, send your e-mail address to **Subscribe@OustAKing.com** or through website above (Contact).

For speaking engagements, radio/TV discussions or other public events, please e-mail requests to **Events@OustAKing.com** or through website above (Contact).

www.ingramcontent.com/pod-product-compliance
Lightning Source LLC
Chambersburg PA
CBHW051617030426
42334CB00030B/3235